THE **CORE** METHOD

THE **CORE** METHOD

THE GUIDE TO PURPOSE DRIVEN RESULTS

NATALIE R. WILLIAMS

Charleston, SC
www.PalmettoPublishing.com

The **CORE** Method
Copyright © 2023 by Natalie R. Williams

Hardcover ISBN: 979-8-8229-3064-3
Paperback ISBN: 979-8-8229-3065-0
eBook ISBN 979-8-8229-2822-0

Table of Contents

Foreword

OUR PURPOSE IS WHAT defines us as human beings. Too often, we drift through the various stages of life never truly realizing our fullest potential. We may have big dreams, hopes, and wishes; however, only those who truly follow their purpose and live in it each day have an opportunity to achieve purpose-driven results.

I wrote *The CORE Method* because I realized at an early age that my purpose is to serve. I have overcome many obstacles by applying The CORE Method in all that I do. My childhood and early adult stages of life weren't ideal. I was born in Raleigh, North Carolina, and raised in Columbia, South Carolina, where my parents divorced when I was a young child. My mother worked hard to provide, which left a lot of room for me to get involved with the wrong crowd. I eventually dropped out of high school and at the age of sixteen-years-old relocated to Atlanta, Georgia, where I endured traumatizing physical and emotional abuse from my significant other at the time. There were many days when I thought my life would come to an end at the hands of my abuser. I had my first child on my eighteenth birthday. I didn't have a high school diploma or any postsecondary education and worked retail jobs while in an abusive living situation. At times, I wanted to give up on life.

I eventually moved back home to South Carolina away from my abuser, where I was able to earn my high school diploma and started my professional career with a Fortune 500 organization. I met my husband—my soulmate and best friend—and we have been married for over twenty years and have three beautiful sons. I had a successful, twenty-four year career filled with many experiences that developed my skill sets and capabilities. I leveraged my employer's tuition assistance program and earned my Bachelor of Business Administration and Master of Public Administration. I dedicated my career to developing teams and getting results.

As a servant leader, I stayed true to my mission of connecting people to purpose. This approach resulted in me being a top performer, and I earned several awards for my results and promotions. Connecting people to purpose was the solution to achieving long-term, sustainable results. I eventually left my career to get closer connected to my purpose.

Today, I am the founder and CEO of The CORE Method LLC, where I specialize in professional development and life coaching services. I work with clients who are also seeking to achieve purpose-driven results. My purpose is to serve—that is the *core* of who I am.

Many ask—how did I overcome such obstacles to be the woman I am today? My answer is simple: I leaned into my purpose and got clear about what I wanted for my life; I optimized every opportunity; I reflected on my actions. Most importantly, I mastered the art of execution.

The CORE Method is how I got my life on track and delivered purpose-driven results. I invite you to take this journey to get connected to your purpose and experience life-changing results.

Thank you for supporting my purpose.

—Natalie R. Williams

CHAPTER 1

Purpose Defined

Foundation of The CORE Method

The CORE Method comprises four distinct principles**:**

- Clarity

- Optimization

- Reflection

- Execution

Purpose is foundational to *The CORE Method* framework. I define purpose as a deliberate choice to achieve a specific result. In a more compelling sense, purpose is a goal or objective that inspires intentional action; purpose is the driving force behind our actions and decisions. It is the reason why we do what we do, and it gives our lives meaning and direction. Having a sense of purpose can help us stay motivated, focused, and fulfilled, even in the face of challenges and setbacks. Fulfilling your purpose is a lifelong journey that often involves exploring your passions, values, and strengths. It is important to take time to reflect on what is truly important to you and to identify the things that give your life meaning. Once you have done so, this knowledge can yield life-changing results.

One of the key benefits of having a sense of purpose is that it can help you stay focused on your goals. When you have a clear sense of purpose, you are more likely to stay committed. Commitment can help you overcome obstacles and achieve your dreams, even in the face of adversity. Having a sense of purpose will help you make better choices and decisions. When you know what is truly important to you, you are better positioned to prioritize your time and energy. It's important in life to ensure that your actions are in alignment with your desired outcomes; doing so can help you live a more fulfilling life and can lead to greater well-being.

As you explore your purpose, it is important to evaluate your personal value system and unique interests—this may involve exploring new opportunities, taking risks, and stepping outside of your comfort zone. It may also involve seeking out mentors or role models who can help guide you on your journey.

Once you have identified and defined your purpose, establish clear objectives, develop a plan of action, and stay accountable to yourself and others. You'll also need to actively seek out support and encouragement from friends, family, a coach, or a mentor.

In this chapter, we will explore the importance of purpose across various spectrums of life.

History of Purpose

Philosophers, theologians, and scientists have all debated the idea of purpose throughout history.

A few examples:

- According to Charles Darwin, who is commonly cited as discovering evolutionary theory, evolution reveals that organisms have a scientific purpose for existing and procreating

- Aristotle believed that the purpose of life is to pursue happiness.

- Rick Warren, the best-selling author of *The Purpose Driven Life*, defines purpose as "the reason you exist." According to Warren, God has predetermined a specific purpose for each person, and he contends that the secret to living a happy and meaningful life is identifying your individual purpose.

- Susan Wolf, a philosopher and professor at the University of North Carolina at Chapel Hill, has written extensively on ethics and the meaning of life. In her book *Meaning in Life and Why It Matters*, Wolf argues that finding purpose requires a sense of connection to something larger than oneself, such as a community, a cause, or a spiritual belief.

- Viktor Frankl was an Austrian neurologist and psychiatrist who survived the Holocaust and went on to develop a form of psychotherapy known as logotherapy. In his book *Man's Search for Meaning*, Frankl argues that finding purpose is essential for human well-being and that individuals can find meaning in even the most difficult circumstances.

As human beings, we are always searching for purpose and meaning in our lives. We want to know that our existence has significance and that we are contributing toward something greater than ourselves. This search for meaning and purpose is a fundamental aspect of our human experience, and it is what drives us to pursue our goals and dreams.

Meaning is the significance or value that we attach to something—without meaning, life can feel empty. We find meaning in a variety of ways: through our relationships, our work, our hobbies, and our spirituality.

Connection to purpose is closely related to finding meaning; purpose is the driving force behind our actions and decisions. When we have a clear sense of purpose, we are more inclined to achieve success and deliver results. Finding meaning and connection to purpose is not always easy—it requires self-reflection and a willingness to challenge your worldview and personal beliefs. It also requires us to be open to new experiences and to be willing to take risks.

One way to find meaning and connection to purpose is to identify our strengths. When we are doing something that we are good at and that we enjoy, we are more likely to feel a sense of purpose and fulfillment. We can also find meaning by helping others and making a positive impact in the world.

Another way to find meaning and connection to purpose is to cultivate a sense of gratitude and appreciation for the present moment. When we are fully present and engaged in the moment, we are more likely to find meaning and purpose in our lives.

Ultimately, finding meaning and connection to purpose is a parallel lifelong journey. It requires us to be open to new experiences, willing to take risks, and committed to personal growth and development. When we are able to find meaning and purpose in our lives, we are more likely to live a fulfilling and meaningful existence.

I took the journey of finding purpose in life as a young adult. As a single mother and domestic violence survivor without any formal education. I often questioned my purpose in life. I questioned my existence and second-guessed my abilities. I had to do the work to gain more confidence. I asked myself the tough questions, examined my personal values, and evaluated my strengths. I committed to always aligning my actions and any future opportunities with my values. I determined that my purpose in life is to serve others. I seek to be a resource for those who are seeking to elevate their lives. I eventually became an executive leader in a Fortune 20 organization. I achieved results for the business by connecting my employees to purpose and meaning. I was very clear and intentional about the goals of the organization and how we would achieve success together as a team. I also invested resources into helping my employees be their personal and professional best selves. My commitment to following my purpose led to a successful career where I enjoyed helping others and getting results.

Purpose and Workplace Culture

Purpose and workplace culture are closely related—a strong sense of purpose can help create a positive workplace culture, while a positive workplace culture can help reinforce a sense of purpose among employees.

Purpose in the workplace is described as the reason why an organization exists and the impact it seeks to make in society. When employees feel that their work is meaningful and aligned with the organization's purpose, they are more likely to be engaged and motivated; this can lead to higher levels of job satisfaction, productivity, and employee retention.

A positive workplace culture supports and encourages employees to thrive. It is characterized by open communication, collaboration, respect, and a shared sense of values. When employees feel that they are part of a supportive and positive workplace culture, they are more likely to feel a sense of belonging and connection to the organization.

One way to create a positive workplace culture that reinforces a sense of purpose is to involve employees in the development and execution of the organization's purpose and values. When employees feel that their input is valued and that they have a say in the direction of the organization, they are more likely to feel invested in its success.

Another way to reinforce a sense of purpose in the workplace is to provide opportunities for employees to connect with the organization's mission and impact—this can include volunteer opportunities, community service projects, or other initiatives that allow employees to see firsthand the positive impact that the organization is making in the world.

Leadership also plays a critical role in creating a workplace culture that reinforces a sense of purpose. Leaders who are transparent, authentic, and committed to the organization's purpose and values are more likely to inspire and motivate employees. They can also help create a culture of trust and accountability, which is essential for a positive workplace culture.

Though organizations aspire to have a positive workplace culture, there are many environments where these aspirations have not been achieved. If you find yourself in an unhealthy workplace culture or toxic leadership environment, it can take a toll on your ability to properly function. You may feel defeated or distracted from pursuing your purpose. These are normal feelings when faced with this type of challenge. If you are faced with a toxic workplace culture, there are steps that you can take to overcome the challenges:

1. **Set boundaries:** Establish clear boundaries between your work and personal life. Avoid bringing work-related stress or negativity home with you. Engage in activities outside of work that help you relax and recharge.

2. **Seek support:** Connect with colleagues who share your concerns about the toxic culture. Having a support system can provide emotional validation and help you navigate the challenges. Consider joining professional networks or seeking mentorship outside of your workplace.

3. **Practice self-care**: Prioritize self-care activities to maintain your well-being. Engage in regular exercise, practice mindfulness or meditation, and ensure you get enough restful sleep. Taking care of your physical and mental health can help you better cope with the toxic environment.

4. **Communicate assertively:** When faced with toxic behavior or situations, practice assertive communication. Clearly

express your concerns, set boundaries, and address issues directly with the individuals involved. Use "I" statements to express how their behavior affects you, and propose potential solutions.

5. **Explore options:** Assess your options for improving the situation. This may include discussing concerns with a supervisor or HR representative, seeking a transfer to a different department or team, or even considering a job change if the toxicity persists and affects your well-being.

Remember, each workplace situation is unique, and it's important to evaluate what strategies are most appropriate for your specific circumstances. Seeking professional advice or guidance from a career counselor or therapist can also be beneficial.

In summary, purpose and workplace culture are closely linked. A strong sense of purpose can help to create a positive workplace culture, while a positive workplace culture can reinforce a sense of purpose among employees. By involving employees in the development of the organization's purpose and values, providing opportunities for employees to connect with the organization's mission and impact, and cultivating authentic and transparent leadership, organizations can create a workplace culture that supports and encourages employees to thrive. These efforts will position the organization to achieve long-term, sustainable results.

Individual Identity and Purpose

Individual identity is a unique set of characteristics that encompasses your personal beliefs, values, and experiences; identity is what defines who we are as individuals; it is what makes us distinct from others and shapes our sense of self. A key component of individual identity is self-awareness. Self-awareness is the ability to recognize and comprehend our thoughts, feelings, and behaviors. It is an important aspect of individual identity because it allows us to understand how our strengths and weaknesses influence our decision-making process.

Another important aspect of individual identity is our sense of belonging. Generally speaking, as human beings, we all need to feel connected to others and that we are part of a community. Our sense of belonging is shaped by our relationships with others, our cultural background, and our shared experiences. Individual identity can also be shaped by our experiences with adversity and challenging circum-stances—adversity can help us develop resilience and perseverance; it can also help us develop a deeper understanding of ourselves.

Our individual identity is not fixed or static—it can change and evolve as we grow and develop. We may experience significant life events or changes in our environment that can impact our sense of self and our identity. One of the challenges of individual identity is balancing our sense of self with our relationships with others. We may feel pressure to conform to the expectations of others or to fit in with a particular group; however, it is important to maintain a sense of authenticity and to stay true to our values and beliefs.

Identity plays a significant role in finding purpose. Our individual identity is reflected in the path of our lives. When we have a clear un-derstanding of our identity, we are better able to take the appropriate actions toward achieving success, resulting in purpose-driven results.

Our experiences shape our perspectives; your individual identity is a direct reflection of your personal value system. Our values are the beliefs and principles that are most important to us—they guide our decision-making and help us determine what is meaningful and important. When we have a clear understanding of our values, we are better able to identify opportunities that align with our purpose.

For example, someone who has experienced a significant loss or hardship may be motivated to pursue a career or activity that helps others who are going through similar circumstances. Our lived ex-periences also help us identify our strengths and motivators, which can guide us toward our purpose.

The more that you understand who you are, the better positioned you are to align your life to meet your fundamental needs. Fulfilling your needs is an important factor when pursuing success. For example, someone who is introverted may be more fulfilled by pursuing a career or activity that allows them to work independently, while someone who is extroverted may be more fulfilled by pursuing a career or activity that involves working with others.

Determining your identity is a complex and ongoing process. Consider the following when evaluating where you are in the process:

- **Self-reflection:** Take time to reflect on your values, beliefs, and experiences. Consider what is most important to you and what motivates and inspires you.

- **Self-awareness:** Develop self-awareness by paying attention to your thoughts, feelings, and behaviors; notice patterns and tendencies that may reveal aspects of your identity.

- **Exploration**: Explore different interests, hobbies, and activities that align with your values and goals. Try new things and step outside of your comfort zone to discover new aspects of yourself.

- **Relationships**: Pay attention to the relationships in your life—notice how you interact with others and how they perceive you. Consider how your relationships reflect your identity.

- **Feedback**: Seek feedback from others who know you well; ask for their honest opinions and perspectives on your strengths, weaknesses, and personality traits.

- **Acceptance:** Accept that your identity is not fixed or static—it may change and evolve as you grow and develop as a person.

In summary, identity plays a significant role in finding your purpose. Your values, experiences, and sense of self-awareness all influence your sense of purpose and direction in life. By understanding your identity and staying true to your values and passions, you can find a sense of fulfillment and purpose in your life. By staying true to your values and beliefs, you can maintain a sense of authenticity and live a fulfilling and meaningful life.

Finding Purpose Is a Journey

Purpose is not a destination that we just arrive at, but rather a journey that we embark on throughout our lives. It is a process of self-discovery, ongoing development, and growth. Purpose is not something that we find, but rather something that we create through our choices and actions.

Practicing mindfulness is a great way to stay centered on your journey. Mindfulness involves being fully engaged and present in the moment, without distraction or preconceived notions. By practicing mindfulness, we can become more aware of our thoughts, feelings, and actions, and make intentional choices. We will revisit mindfulness in more depth in Chapter 2.

As a journey, purpose requires practice and commitment—it is not something we can achieve overnight, but rather something we must consistently work toward over time. This involves setting goals, taking action, and reflecting on our progress and experiences. Self-reflection involves identifying areas where we can grow and improve.

By reflecting on our experiences, we can gain insight into what works well and perhaps where we need to improve. It's also an opportunity to identify our perceptions of fear and, more importantly, how we respond when there is a perceived threat.

Fear is a natural emotion that is triggered by a perceived threat or danger; it is a basic survival mechanism that helps us respond and protect ourselves from harm. Fear can be experienced in response to a variety of stimuli, including physical danger, social situations, and psychological stressors. When we experience fear, our body responds by releasing adrenaline and other stress hormones, which prepare us for a fight or flight response; this can lead to physical symptoms such as increased heart rate, rapid breathing, and sweating.

Fear can be both helpful and harmful. In some situations, fear can help us respond quickly and effectively to potential threats. For example, if we are walking alone at night and hear footsteps behind us, fear can help us be alert and take action to protect ourselves.

However, fear can also be harmful when it is excessive or irrational. When we experience intense or persistent fear in response to situations that are not actually dangerous, it can interfere with our daily lives and lead to anxiety disorders or phobias. Overcoming fear often involves facing our fears and gradually exposing ourselves to the situations or stimuli that trigger our fear—this can help us to develop a sense of control and reduce our anxiety over time.

Adversity can create fear in life by triggering our natural survival instincts. When we face adversity, our brain perceives a threat and activates the fight or flight response, which prepares us to respond to potential barriers—this can lead to feelings of stress. Adversity can take many forms, including physical, emotional, and psychological challenges. For example, someone who has experienced a traumatic event, such as a car accident or natural disaster, may develop a fear of similar situations. Similarly, someone who has experienced rejection or failure may develop a fear of taking risks or trying new things. Adversity can also create fear by undermining our sense of control and security—when we face unexpected challenges or setbacks, we may feel powerless and vulnerable.

Your ability to effectively overcome fear will be advantageous in the long-term journey of connecting with your purpose in life. When you can respond to adversity with resilience and adaptability, you will view challenges as opportunities for growth and learning. Overcoming fear in the face of adversity often involves developing coping strategies and seeking support from others—this may involve seeking professional help, such as therapy or counseling, or engaging in self-care activities such as exercise, meditation, or creative expression.

Fear can stifle progress toward achieving purpose-driven results in many ways:

- **Avoidance and inaction:** When we are afraid of failure, rejection, or uncertainty, we may avoid taking risks or pursuing our goals; this can prevent us from making progress toward our purpose and limit our potential for growth and development.

- **Self-doubt and negative self-talk:** We may question our abilities and worthiness and engage in negative self-talk that undermines our confidence and motivation; this can make it difficult to stay focused on our purpose and take the necessary steps to achieve our goals.

- **Narrow focus and limited perspective:** We may become overly focused on potential threats or obstacles and overlook opportunities for growth and learning; this can limit our creativity and innovation, and prevent us from exploring new ideas and approaches that could help us achieve our purpose.

- **Lack of resilience and adaptability:** When we are afraid, we may become rigid and inflexible in our thinking and behavior, and resist change or uncertainty; this can make it difficult to adapt to new challenges and opportunities and limit our ability to achieve our purpose in a changing world.

Overcoming fear can be a challenging but worthwhile process. When I am faced with fear, I leverage the following seven strategies to get back on track and position myself to take action:

1. **Identify the fear:** Identify the specific fear that you are experiencing; this can help you understand the root cause of your fear and develop a plan to address it.

2. **Challenge negative thoughts:** Challenge negative thoughts and beliefs that may be contributing to your fear. Replace them with positive and realistic thoughts that can help you to feel more confident and empowered.

3. **Take small steps:** Take small steps toward facing your fear; this can help you to build confidence and gradually overcome your fear.

4. **Practice relaxation techniques:** Practice relaxation techniques such as deep breathing, meditation, or yoga—these techniques can help you manage the anxiety and stress associated with fear.

5. **Seek support:** Seek support from friends, family, or a professional counselor. Talking about your fear with someone you trust can help you gain perspective and develop coping strategies.

6. **Visualize success:** Visualize yourself successfully over-coming your fear; this can help you build confidence and motivation to take action.

7. **Take action:** Take action toward facing your fear—this can be challenging, but taking action is often the most effective way to overcome fear.

Don't allow fear to limit your potential. Lean into your capabilities and focus on what you can control.

Maria's Journey to Purpose

I once worked with a client who is a perfect example of how to over-come life's challenges and stay the course of fulfilling purpose. Maria is a single mother who has faced many obstacles in her life. She grew up in a low-income neighborhood and struggled to make ends meet for most of her life. Maria wanted to provide a better life for her daughter. She worked long hours at a minimum wage job, but she always felt like she was barely keeping her head above water.

One day, Maria decided that she had enough—she realized that she wanted to create a better life for herself and her daughter and that she needed to take action if she wanted to achieve her goals. Maria started by going back to school to get her degree. She knew that education was the key to unlocking better job opportunities and creating a better life for her family.

Despite the challenges of being a single mother and working full-time, Maria was determined to succeed. She spent countless hours studying and attending classes, and she even started a side business selling handmade crafts to make extra money. As she continued to work hard and pursue her goals, Maria faced many setbacks and obstacles. She struggled to balance her responsibilities as a mother and a student, and she faced financial challenges that threatened to derail her progress. But Maria refused to give up—she was driven by her love for her daughter and her desire to create a better life for her family. She continued to work hard and persevere through the challenges, and eventually, her hard work paid off.

Maria graduated with honors and landed a job at a prestigious company in her field. She was able to provide a better life for her daughter, and she even started a nonprofit organization to help other single mothers achieve their goals.

Through her journey of overcoming adversity, Maria learned that true success and fulfillment come from pursuing her goals and living a purpose-driven life, even in the face of challenges and setbacks. By refusing to give up and staying true to her values and priorities, Maria was able to achieve purpose-driven results and create a better life for herself and her family.

Conclusion

Defining purpose can have many advantages for individuals and organizations. Purpose is an essential component of human existence and is crucial to our well-being and sense of fulfillment. Purpose gives us a sense of direction and meaning, which can reduce feelings of anxiety, stress, and overwhelm. Furthermore, having a clearly defined purpose has been linked to improved cognitive function and resilience, which can enhance our ability to solve problems and make decisions. When we have a clear sense of purpose, we are more likely to feel fulfilled and content, even in adversity.

Organizations with a strong sense of purpose are more likely to attract and retain talented employees committed to their mission and values. Additionally, purpose-driven organizations are more likely to create positive social and environmental impacts, which can contribute to their long-term success. Creating a culture that emphasizes purpose and meaning in work can improve performance, productivity, and innovation.

Additionally, life experiences and events can impact our sense of purpose, so it is critical to be adaptable and open to changes over time; it also requires ongoing self-reflection, introspection, and a willingness to explore new ideas and possibilities. The benefits of defining purpose are well worth the effort, as we can experience a greater quality of life. Finding purpose can be difficult, as it may require us to face questions about our fundamental values, beliefs, strengths, and opportunities—it is necessary to engage in self-reflection to determine our purpose.

What is meaningful and purposeful to one person may not be the same for another, and ultimately, defining purpose is a deeply personal and individual process. Nevertheless, by exploring and defining our purpose, we can lead more fulfilling lives for ourselves and help bring about positive change in the world. The CORE Method will guide you along your journey of fulfilling purpose-driven results.

A MOMENT OF REFLECTION

1. **What are your core values?**

_____

_____

_____

2. **What motivates you?**

_____

_____

_____

3. **What is your identity?**

_____

_____

_____

_____

4. Imagine you at your "best" possible self. What do you see? How can you get closer to being your best self?

_____

_____

_____

5. What do you believe is your purpose?

_____

_____

_____

6. Why is it important to you?

_____

_____

_____

7. Are you living for your purpose? If not, what's stopping you?

_____

_____

_____

CHAPTER 2

Clarity

CLARITY IS THE STATE of being clear, transparent, and easily understood. Clarity applies to many aspects of life. Most notably, clarity is foundational to our ability to effectively communicate, establish goals, and strengthen our decision-making skills.

- **Communication:** Communication is the ability to express yourself clearly and effectively and to understand others' messages clearly; this involves using clear and concise language, avoiding ambiguity and confusion, and actively listening to others to ensure mutual understanding.

- **Goal setting:** Goal setting means you create a clear and specific vision of what you want to achieve and develop a plan to achieve it; this involves setting clear and measurable goals, identifying the steps needed to achieve them, and tracking progress toward them.

- **Decision-making:** Decision-making requires a clear understanding of your goals, values, and priorities, and using this understanding to make informed and effective decisions; this involves gathering information, weighing options, and considering the potential consequences of your choices.

Clarity is important because it helps us to communicate effectively, make informed decisions, and achieve our goals. When we have clarity, we are better able to understand ourselves and others and better able to take action toward our desired outcomes. Let's explore key concepts and strategies for achieving clarity in how we communicate, make decisions, and establish goals.

Communication

Communication is essential for building and maintaining relationships with others. It allows us to connect with others, share our thoughts and feelings, and build trust and understanding. Effective communication allows us to express ourselves and share our ideas, opinions, and emotions with others—this can help us feel heard and understood and help us connect with others on a deeper level. Conflict is a natural occurrence in life. Our ability to effectively resolve conflict is contingent on our ability to communicate. Effective communication allows us to express our concerns, listen to others' perspectives, and work together to find mutually beneficial solutions.

Sharing knowledge and ideas, asking questions, and receiving feedback are all forms of communication that allow room for learning and growth; practicing these tools can help us expand our understanding and develop new perspectives while achieving our goals. Communication is important for achieving our goals, both personally and professionally. It allows us to share our vision and ideas with others, collaborate effectively, and work toward a common mission.

Achieving clarity in communication involves six critical strategies:

1. **Use clear and concise language:** Use simple, straightforward language that is easy to understand. Avoid using

jargon, technical terms, or complex sentences that may confuse the listener.

2. **Be specific:** Provide specific details and examples to illustrate your point; this can help you clarify your message and make it more concrete and understandable.

3. **Use active listening:** Listen actively to the other person's response and ask questions to ensure mutual understanding; this can help to clarify any misunderstandings and ensure that both parties are on the same page.

4. **Avoid assumptions:** Avoid making assumptions about what the other person knows or understands. Instead, ask questions and seek clarification to ensure you are both on the same page.

5. **Use visual aids:** Use visual aids such as diagrams, charts, or graphs to help illustrate your point; this can help you clarify complex ideas and make them more understandable.

6. **Check for understanding:** Check for understanding by summarizing your message and asking the other person to repeat it back to you; this can help you ensure that your message has been understood correctly.

By improving your communication skills, you can enhance your personal and professional relationships, and achieve greater success in purpose-driven results.

Goal Setting

Setting goals provides direction and focus. It helps you identify what you want to achieve and the steps you need to take to get there. Having goals can also be a powerful motivator—goals give you something to work toward and help you stay focused and committed to your efforts.

It is also beneficial to establish a vision statement. A vision statement describes your long-term aspirations and goals; it outlines what you hope to achieve in the future and provides a clear direction for decision-making and goal setting. A vision statement is often used as a motivational tool to inspire and guide individuals or teams toward a common goal. It should be concise, memorable, and inspiring, and should reflect your core values and beliefs.

Measuring progress against your goals is critical. Goals provide a way to measure progress and track achievements; this can help you adjust as needed to stay on track. Tracking your progress also increases your self-confidence and self-esteem—it shows you that you are capable of achieving what you set out to do and can help you overcome self-doubt and fear.

Setting goals can also contribute to making optimized decisions. It allows you to consider your options and weigh the potential outcomes of different choices. Setting and achieving goals can enhance personal growth and development. It allows you to learn new skills, gain new experiences, and expand your knowledge and understanding of the world.

Here are seven methods for gaining clarity through goal setting:

1. **Craft a vision statement:** The best approach to writing a vision statement involves considering your long-term aspirations, reflecting on your core values and beliefs, and creating a concise, memorable, and inspiring statement that

provides a clear direction for decision-making and goal setting. It is important to involve key stakeholders in the process, use clear and simple language, and ensure that the statement is realistic and achievable. The vision statement should be revisited regularly to ensure that it remains relevant and aligned with your goals and values.

2. **Define your goals:** Start by defining your goals clearly and specifically; this involves identifying what you want to achieve, why it is important to you, and what steps you need to take to achieve it.

3. **Make your goals measurable:** Make your goals measurable by setting specific targets and deadlines; this can help you track your progress and stay motivated.

4. **Break down your goals into smaller steps:** Break down your goals into smaller, more manageable steps; this can help you stay focused and motivated to make progress toward your goals more easily.

5. **Prioritize your goals:** Prioritize your goals based on their importance and urgency; this can help you focus your time and energy on the most important goals and achieve them more quickly.

6. **Write down your goals:** Write down your goals and keep them in a visible place; this can help you stay focused and motivated and remind you of what you are working toward.

7. **Review and adjust your goals regularly:** Review your goals regularly and adjust them as needed; this can help you stay on track and make progress toward your goals more effectively.

Another proven and widely utilized framework is the SMART goal-setting process. SMART is an acronym that stands for specific, measurable, achievable, relevant, and time-bound. Here's a breakdown of each component:

- **Specific:** Avoid vague or general statements. Clearly define what you want to achieve, including the who, what, where, when, and why. The more specific your goal, the easier it is to create a plan and take action.

- **Measurable:** Goals should be measurable so that progress can be tracked and evaluated. Establish concrete criteria or indicators to assess your progress. This allows you to determine if you are on track and motivates you as you see measurable results.

- **Achievable:** Consider your resources, skills, and limitations when setting goals. Goals should be realistic and attainable. It's important to set challenging goals, but they should also be within your reach. Setting unattainable goals can lead to frustration and demotivation.

- **Relevant:** Goals should be relevant and aligned with your overall objectives and values. Ensure that your goals are meaningful and contribute to your personal or professional growth. Aligning your goals with your broader aspirations increases motivation and commitment.

- **Time-bound:** Identify specific timeframes or deadlines. This helps create a sense of urgency and provides a timeline for action. Setting deadlines helps you stay focused and accountable, preventing procrastination.

By applying the SMART criteria to your goal-setting process, you can increase the likelihood of success. It helps you clarify your objectives, track progress, stay motivated, and make adjustments as needed. Remember to regularly review and reassess your goals to ensure they remain relevant and aligned with your evolving needs and circumstances.

Decision-Making

Decision-making is important because it helps you clarify your goals and priorities. When you make decisions, you are forced to consider your options and weigh the potential outcomes and or consequences of each choice—this process can help you gain clarity about what you truly want and what is most important to you.

For example, if you are trying to decide between two job offers, the decision-making process can help you to clarify your career goals and priorities. You may consider factors such as salary, job responsibilities, work-life balance, and opportunities for growth and development. By weighing these factors and making a decision, you can gain clarity about what you want in a career and what is most important.

Similarly, decision-making can help you clarify your values and beliefs. When you are faced with difficult choices, you may need to consider your ethical or moral principles and weigh them against other factors.

Here are seven steps for effective decision-making:

1. **Define the problem:** Start by defining the problem or decision you need to make; this involves identifying the key issues, factors, and stakeholders involved.

2. **Gather information:** Gather information about the problem or decision from a variety of sources; this can include research, data, expert opinions, and feedback from others.

3. **Identify options:** Identify a range of options or solutions to the problem or decision; this can involve brainstorming, considering different perspectives, and evaluating the pros and cons of each option.

4. **Evaluate options:** Evaluate each option based on its potential outcomes, risks, and benefits. Consider how each option aligns with your goals, values, and priorities.

5. **Make a decision:** Make a decision based on the information and analysis you have gathered. Choose the option that best aligns with your goals, values, and priorities.

6. **Take action:** Take action to implement your decision; this may involve developing a plan, communicating your decision to others, and taking steps to achieve your desired outcomes.

7. **Reflect and learn:** Reflect on the decision-making process and the outcomes of your decision. Consider what worked well and what could be improved for future decisions.

By using these strategies, you can make more informed decisions that align with your goals, values, and priorities, and achieve greater clarity and success.

Define Success

Now, let's explore how defining success will assist with achieving clarity. When we have mental clarity, we can think clearly and focus our attention on the present moment, which can help us make better decisions and achieve our desired outcomes.

Mental clarity can also help with developing greater self-awareness and emotional intelligence. Emotional intelligence is the ability to recognize, understand, and manage emotions. It involves being aware of and able to regulate your emotions, as well as being able to empathize with and respond appropriately to the emotions of others. Emotional intelligence is often considered a key factor in personal and professional success, as it can help you navigate social situations, build strong relationships, and communicate effectively. When we can understand our thoughts and emotions, we are better equipped to communicate effectively with others and build strong, supportive relationships.

The definition of success can vary depending on an individual's values, goals, and priorities. Generally, success is defined as the achievement of a desired outcome or goal; however, success can also be subjective and can mean different things to different people. For some, success may be defined by financial wealth or career achievements. For others, success may be defined by personal relationships, health, or happiness. Success can also be defined as making a positive impact on the world or contributing to a greater cause.

Defining success can help us avoid comparing ourselves to others or measuring our success against external standards. When we have our own definition of success, we are less likely to be swayed by societal pressures or the expectations of others and more likely to live a life that is true to our values and priorities.

Ultimately, success is a personal and subjective matter that can vary greatly from person to person. We need to define success for ourselves based on our values and priorities, rather than relying on external measures of success; this will be important to our journey because we must be confident in our ability to achieve desired outcomes.

I define success upfront in any endeavor that I am serious about achieving. I identify what is possible and establish milestones for the project or initiative. I celebrate small wins and identify potential roadblocks and barriers. I am clear about the intended outcomes and consistently evaluate progress toward the end results. I find that establishing this early in the process ensures that I stay committed to the course.

Practice Mindfulness

In Chapter 1, we briefly discussed mindfulness as a factor in determining your life's purpose. Mindfulness is a mental state of awareness, focus, and acceptance of the present moment. It involves paying attention to your thoughts, feelings, and physical sensations without judgment or distraction. Mindfulness is often associated with meditation practices, but it can also be practiced in daily routines.

Mindfulness can help you gain clarity in life by increasing your self-awareness and ability to focus on the present moment. When you practice mindfulness, you learn to observe your thoughts and emotions without judgment or distraction—this can help you gain a deeper understanding of your thought patterns and behaviors, which can lead to greater clarity.

By practicing mindfulness, you can also learn to let go of negative thought patterns that can cloud your judgment and prevent you from seeing situations for what they are. The ultimate goal is to leverage your knowledge to make more informed decisions and take actions that are aligned with accomplishing your goals.

Below are three mindfulness techniques that can help you gain clarity:

1. **Mindful breathing:** Mindful breathing is a simple yet powerful technique that can help you focus your attention and calm your mind. To practice mindful breathing, find a quiet place where you can sit comfortably. Close your eyes

and take a few deep breaths, focusing on the sensation of the air moving in and out of your body. Then, allow your breath to settle into its natural rhythm and simply observe it without trying to control it. If your mind wanders, gently bring your attention back to your breath.

2. **Body scan meditation:** Body scan meditation is a technique that involves systematically focusing your attention on different parts of your body, moving from your toes to the top of your head. This technique can help you become more aware of physical sensations and release tension and stress. To practice body scan meditation, lie down or sit in a comfortable position and close your eyes. Begin by focusing on your breath for a few minutes, then slowly move your attention to your toes. Notice any sensations you feel in your toes, then move your attention up to your feet, ankles, and so on, until you have scanned your entire body.

3. **Mindful journaling:** Mindful journaling involves writing down your thoughts and feelings in a nonjudgmental way. This technique can help you gain clarity by allowing you to explore your thoughts and emotions without getting caught up in them. To practice mindful journaling, find a quiet place where you can write without distractions. Set a timer for ten to fifteen minutes and begin writing whatever comes to mind, without worrying about grammar or spelling. If you get stuck, try writing down a question or prompt to help guide your thoughts. When the timer goes off, take a few deep breaths and read over what you have written, noticing any patterns or insights that emerge.

Mindfulness can help you develop a greater sense of compassion and empathy for yourself and others—this can help you navigate difficult situations with greater clarity and understanding and can lead to more positive and fulfilling relationships. Mindfulness can be a very powerful tool for gaining clarity in life by helping you develop greater self-awareness, focus, and compassion. By practicing mindfulness regularly, you can cultivate a deeper sense of clarity and purpose in your life.

There are several online applications available that can help you practice mindfulness. Here are three popular ones:

1. **Headspace** is a widely recognized mindfulness app that offers guided meditation and mindfulness exercises. It provides a variety of themed meditation sessions, including stress reduction, sleep improvement, and focus enhancement. The app offers both free and subscription-based content, making it accessible to users at different levels of mindfulness practice.

2. **Calm** is another popular mindfulness app that offers guided meditations, sleep stories, breathing exercises, and relaxing music. It provides a range of mindfulness programs designed to reduce anxiety, improve sleep, and enhance overall well-being. Calm offers a free version with limited content and a subscription-based model for access to the full range of features.

3. **Insight Timer** is a free mindfulness app that offers a vast library of guided meditations, talks, and music tracks from various teachers and practitioners. It provides a customizable meditation timer, allowing users to set their preferred duration and background sounds. Insight Timer also offers a community aspect, allowing users to connect with others and join meditation groups.

These apps are available for download on both iOS and Android devices. It's worth exploring each app to find the one that resonates most with your preferences and needs. Additionally, many mindfulness teachers and organizations offer their own apps or online platforms, so it can be beneficial to explore different options to find the resources that work best for you.

I also offer mindfulness as a component of The CORE Method coaching program. You can learn more by visiting TheCOREMethodLLC.com

How Sarah Achieved Purpose-Driven Results by Gaining Clarity

I worked with a client named Sarah who is an entrepreneur with a passion for creating sustainable products that make a positive impact on the environment. Sarah has always been interested in environmental issues and has a deep commitment to creating a better world for future generations.

When Sarah decided to start her own business, she knew that she would need to use effective communication, goal setting, decision-making, mindfulness, and defining success to achieve purpose-driven results.

Sarah started by assembling a team of talented individuals who shared her passion for sustainability and her commitment to making a positive impact. She made sure that everyone on her team was aligned with the company's mission and values, and she encouraged open communication and collaboration. Together, Sarah and her team set ambitious goals for the company, focusing on creating products that would be environmentally friendly and sustainable. They used data-driven decision-making to prioritize their projects and allocate resources effectively.

Throughout the process, Sarah made sure to communicate clearly and effectively with her team, keeping everyone informed about the company's progress and goals. She encouraged feedback and input from her team members, and she made sure that everyone felt valued and heard.

Sarah also practiced mindfulness, taking time each day to reflect on her goals and priorities and to stay focused on her purpose-driven mission. She made sure to take care of herself and her team, promoting a healthy work-life balance and creating a positive work environment.

As the company grew, Sarah faced many challenges and setbacks. She had to make difficult decisions about resource allocation and product development, and she had to navigate the complexities of the business world—but through it all, Sarah remained committed to her purpose-driven mission. She continued to communicate openly and honestly with her team, setting clear goals and priorities and making data-driven decisions. She also defined success on her own terms, focusing on creating a positive impact on the environment rather than just maximizing profits.

In the end, Sarah's hard work and dedication paid off. Her company creates sustainable products that make a positive impact on the environment, and she was able to achieve purpose-driven results as an entrepreneur.

Through her journey, Sarah learned that effective communication, goal setting, decision-making, mindfulness, and defining success are essential skills for any entrepreneur who wants to achieve purpose-driven results. By staying true to her values and priorities, and by working collaboratively with her team, Sarah was able to create a successful business that makes a positive impact on the world and aligned to her purpose.

Conclusion

Ultimately having clarity gets you closer to fulfilling your purpose; clarity helps you focus on what is most important and relevant to your purpose. It allows you to identify the key actions and steps you need to take to achieve your goals. It provides motivation and inspiration to pursue your purpose. It helps you to stay committed and focused on your goals, even when faced with challenges or setbacks.

Your actions and decisions should align with your intended purpose. Clarity will give you confidence in your abilities and decisions. It allows you to trust yourself and your intuition and make choices that are in line with your purpose and goals. Clarity helps you hold yourself accountable for your actions and decisions. It allows you to measure your progress and success and make adjustments as needed to stay on track. By gaining clarity about your purpose and goals, you can take purposeful action toward achieving your desired outcomes and living a fulfilling life.

A MOMENT OF REFLECTION

Are you an effective communicator? If yes, why? Where do you have opportunities to improve?

_____

_____

_____

What is your personal vision statement?

_____

_____

_____

Write three goals that support your vision and purpose.

_____

_____

_____

_____

What is your definition of success?

_____

_____

_____

_____

What decisions do you need to make to achieve your desired outcome?

_____

_____

_____

_____

Are you actively practicing mindfulness techniques? Identify a method that you haven't tried and commit to implementing into your routine.

_____

_____

_____

_____

_____

CHAPTER 3

Optimization

"You must believe to achieve."
—Harry Hoover

THE PHRASE "YOU MUST BELIEVE TO ACHIEVE" is a popular motivational saying that suggests having a positive mindset and belief in yourself is essential for achieving success. The idea behind this phrase is that if you believe in yourself and your abilities, you are more likely to take action toward your goals and persist in the face of obstacles.

Believing in yourself is a powerful force that can help you overcome self-doubt and fear of failure. When you believe in yourself, you are more likely to take risks, try new things, and push yourself out of your comfort zone—this can lead to personal growth and development, as well as increased confidence and self-esteem.

However, it is important to note that belief alone is not enough to achieve success; belief must be accompanied by action and effort. Simply believing that you can achieve something without taking any action toward that goal is unlikely to lead to success. It is important to set clear goals, develop a plan of action, and take consistent steps toward those goals.

Your Mindset Matters

Optimism and growth mindset are the equivalents of "mind over matter." Optimism is having a positive outlook on life. You expect good things to happen and focus on the positive aspects of situations; it is a mindset that emphasizes hope, confidence, and resilience. Optimism is not the same as denying or ignoring problems—rather, it involves acknowledging difficulties and obstacles while maintaining a belief that things will ultimately work out for the best. Optimistic people tend to view setbacks as temporary and solvable, rather than permanent and insurmountable.

Research has shown that optimism is associated with a range of positive outcomes, including better physical and mental health, increased happiness and life satisfaction, and greater success in achieving goals. Research conducted by Tindle et al. (2009) found that individuals with higher levels of optimism had a reduced risk of developing cardiovascular disease. The study followed over 97,000 women for eight years and concluded that optimism was independently associated with a lower risk of heart disease and other causes of mortality.

A study conducted by Rasmussen et al. (2009) examined the relationship between optimism and mental health in a sample of 5,000 adults. The findings revealed that individuals with higher levels of optimism had lower levels of depression and anxiety. Optimistic individuals were also more likely to engage in positive coping strategies and had higher life satisfaction levels.

A longitudinal study conducted by Segerstrom et al. (2011) followed a group of law students over three years to examine the impact of optimism on academic and professional success. The results showed that students with higher levels of optimism had higher GPAs, were more likely to pass the bar exam, and secured better job offers after graduation. Optimism was found to be a significant predictor of success, even when controlling for other factors such as intelligence and prior academic achievement.

Optimistic individuals tend to have stronger social support networks and cope better with stress. When faced with challenges or setbacks, optimistic individuals are more likely to view them as opportunities for growth and learning. An optimistic mindset can develop adaptability, which is an important skill for navigating life's ups and downs.

Optimism can be cultivated through a variety of practices, such as positive self-talk, gratitude, and mindfulness. By focusing on the positive aspects of situations and reframing negative thoughts, individuals can develop a more optimistic outlook on life. Additionally, seeking out positive experiences and surrounding yourself with supportive people can help reinforce an optimistic mindset.

It is important to note that optimism is not a panacea for all of life's problems: there will always be challenges and setbacks, and it is natural to experience negative emotions at times.

However, cultivating an optimistic mindset can help you develop the resilience and coping skills needed to navigate inevitable challenges and emerge stronger on the other side. Optimism is imperative when seeking to establish a growth mindset.

A growth mindset is the belief that your abilities and intelligence can be developed through hard work, dedication, and perseverance; this mindset emphasizes the importance of effort and learning from mistakes rather than innate talent or intelligence. Developing a growth mindset can help you be more resilient and adaptable. Additionally, a growth mindset can help you develop a sense of purpose and motivation, as you focus on developing your skills and achieving your goals.

Professionally, a growth mindset can be a valuable asset in the workplace. By emphasizing the importance of effort and learning, you can develop the skills needed to succeed in your career—this mindset can help you develop a sense of curiosity and tenacity, which can also lead to professional growth and development. A growth mindset is a useful skill to develop in any career path.

One of the key benefits of a growth mindset is its ability to help you overcome self-doubt and fear of failure. By viewing mistakes and setbacks as opportunities for growth and learning, you can develop a more positive outlook on your abilities and potential—this can lead to increased confidence and self-esteem, which can have a positive impact on both your personal and professional life.

In summary, cultivating a growth mindset requires a willingness to embrace challenges and view mistakes as opportunities for growth. It also requires a commitment to learning and self-improvement, as you must be willing to put in the effort needed to develop your skills and achieve your goals. By developing a growth mindset, you can unlock your full potential and achieve success, both personally and professionally.

Here are seven beneficial strategies for developing a growth mindset:

1. **Embrace challenges:** Don't avoid challenges. Seek out opportunities to learn and grow. Embracing challenges can help you develop new skills and build resilience in the face of setbacks.

2. **View mistakes as opportunities for growth:** Rather than seeing mistakes as failures, view them as opportunities to learn and improve. Reflect on what went wrong and what you can do differently next time.

3. **Focus on effort and progress:** Focus on the effort you put in and the progress you make versus focusing solely on the outcomes. Celebrate small wins and recognize the effort you put in, even if you don't achieve your desired outcome.

4. **Cultivate a love of learning:** Develop curiosity and a willingness to learn new things. Seek out new experiences and opportunities to learn, whether it's through reading, taking courses, or trying new hobbies.

5. **Surround yourself with positive influences:** Surround yourself with people who support and encourage your growth. Seek out mentors and role models who embody a growth mindset and can offer guidance and support.

6. **Practice positive self-talk:** Develop a positive inner dialogue that reinforces your belief in your abilities and potential. Replace negative self-talk with positive affirmations that focus on your strengths and potential.

7. **Emphasize the power of "yet":** When faced with a challenge or setback, add the word "yet" to the end of your statement. For example, "I haven't mastered this skill yet." This simple shift in language can help you view challenges as opportunities for growth and development.

By incorporating these strategies into your daily life, you can develop a growth mindset that will help you achieve your goals and unlock your full potential.

Having optimism and a growth mindset can create an environment that is conducive to optimization and achieving results. Optimism involves having a positive outlook on life and expecting good things to happen, while a growth mindset involves believing that your abilities and intelligence can be developed through hard work and dedication. Together, these mindsets can create a sense of possibility and motivation that can drive you to optimize your performance and achieve your goals.

Optimism and Growth Mindset in the Workplace

Optimism and a growth mindset can have a significant impact on the workplace, both in terms of individual performance and overall organizational success.

Optimistic employees and those with a growth mindset tend to be more motivated and engaged in their work. They are more likely to approach challenges with a sense of possibility and leverage more opportunities for growth and learning. They are more focused and productive. You typically find these employees to be more creative and innovative. There is more willingness to think outside the box and come up with new ideas and solutions to problems, and there is better teamwork with collaboration, sharing of ideas, and general support of colleagues.

The Process of Optimization

Optimization is the process of maximizing efficiency and effectiveness to achieve the best possible results. In the context of personal and professional careers, optimization involves identifying areas for improvement and taking steps to enhance performance and achieve desired outcomes. Optimization also includes setting goals and developing strategies to achieve them.

For example, if an individual wants to improve their physical fitness, they will optimize their workout routine by incorporating new exercises, increasing the intensity of their workouts, or adjusting their diet to support their fitness goals. By optimizing their approach to fitness, they can achieve better results and improve their overall health and well-being.

Professionally, an employee may optimize their work processes by streamlining tasks, delegating responsibilities, or seeking out training and development opportunities to improve their skills. By optimizing their approach to work, they can achieve better results and advance their career.

One clear benefit of optimization is its ability to help you achieve your goals more efficiently and effectively. By identifying areas for improvement and taking steps to enhance performance, you can achieve better results in less time and with less effort. Additionally, optimization will help you develop your sense of purpose and motivation as you focus on achieving your goals and improving your performance.

However, it is important to note that optimization should not come at the expense of personal well-being or work-life balance; it is important to maintain a healthy balance between work and personal life and to prioritize self-care and well-being in the pursuit of optimization.

Let's explore practical ways you can use to optimize your performance and achieve purpose-driven results.

Evaluate Your Strengths

Identifying your strengths is important for accomplishing optimization because it allows you to focus your efforts on areas where you excel and where you can make the greatest impact. It's important to focus on what you do best—by identifying your strengths, you can focus your efforts on activities that align with your skills and interests; this can help you work more efficiently and effectively and achieve better results.

Knowing your strengths can also help you identify areas where you may need to improve. By understanding your strengths and weaknesses, you can develop a plan for personal growth and development that will help you optimize your performance. You will feel more confident in your abilities; you will overcome self-doubt and take on new challenges with a greater sense of ease and enthusiasm. Leveraging your strengths assists you with collaborating more effectively and you can fully contribute and work more successfully with others. By focusing on your strengths, you can prioritize activities that help you make better decisions about how to allocate your time and resources.

Below are a few tips for identifying your strengths:

1. **Self-reflection:** Take some time to reflect on your experiences and accomplishments. Think about the tasks and activities that you enjoy and excel at, and consider the feedback you have received from others—this can help you identify your natural talents and strengths.

2. **Feedback from others:** Ask friends, family members, colleagues, or mentors for feedback on your strengths. They may be able to provide insights that you haven't considered, and their feedback can help you gain a more complete understanding of your strengths.

3. **Personality assessments:** Take a personality assessment, such as the Myers-Briggs Type Indicator—this type of assessment can help you identify your personality traits and strengths and provide insights into how you can leverage them to achieve your goals.

4. **Skill assessments:** Take a skills assessment, such as the CliftonStrengths assessment. Skills assessments can help you identify your natural talents and skills and provide guidance on how to develop and leverage them.

5. **Trial and error:** Try new activities and tasks to see what you enjoy and excel at. This can help you identify your strengths and interests, and provide opportunities for personal growth and development.

By using one or more of these methods, you can gain a better understanding of your strengths and how to leverage them to achieve your goals.

Develop a Plan

Developing a plan is a critical step in achieving personal optimization. It helps you identify your goals, break them down into smaller manageable tasks, and create a timeline for completing them. In Chapter 2, we discussed the goal-setting process. Apply your specific goals toward the initial steps in developing a plan of action. Be very clear about what you want to achieve and the specific purpose.

Once you have defined your goals, the next step is to develop a strategy for achieving them; this involves identifying the steps you need to take to reach your goals, the resources you will need, and the timeline for completing each step.

Create a timeline for completing your tasks. Be realistic and give yourself enough time to complete each task. Prioritize your tasks based on their importance and urgency—this will help you stay focused and ensure that you are making progress toward your goals. Regularly review your plan and adjust it as needed. Reflect on your progress and make adjustments to your plan to ensure that you are being effective and making progress toward achieving the success you have defined.

Time Management

Time management is a critical component of personal optimization. It involves managing your time effectively to achieve your goals and maximize your productivity. In this context, personal optimization refers to the process of improving your personal and professional life to achieve your purpose-driven results. Effective time management can help you stay organized, focused, and motivated on your journey toward personal optimization.

Here are six steps for effective time management:

1. **Identify your priorities:** The first step in effective time management is to identify your priorities. What are the most important tasks that you need to complete? What are your goals? By identifying your priorities, you can focus your time and energy on the tasks that will help you achieve your goals.

2. **Create a schedule:** Once you have identified your priorities, create a schedule. This will help you to manage your time effectively and ensure that you are making progress toward your goals. Be realistic when creating your schedule and give yourself enough time to complete each task.

3. **Use a planner:** A planner is a useful tool for time management. Use it to keep track of your schedule, deadlines, and important tasks; this will help you stay organized and ensure that you are not forgetting anything important.

4. **Avoid distractions:** Distractions can be a major obstacle to effective time management. Identify the things that distract you and try to avoid them—this may involve turning off your phone, closing your email, or working in a quiet space.

5. **Take breaks:** Taking breaks is important for effective time management. It allows you to recharge and refocus, which can help you be more productive in the long run. Take short breaks throughout the day and longer breaks when you need them.

6. **Review and adjust:** Regularly review and adjust your schedule. Reflect on your progress and make adjustments to your schedule to ensure that you are on track to achieve

your goals; this will help you stay organized, focused, and motivated on your journey toward personal optimization. Achieving progress also bolsters self-esteem.

Identify an Accountability Partner

An accountability partner is someone who helps you stay on track and achieve your goals. In the context of achieving personal optimization, an accountability partner can be a valuable tool for staying motivated and accountable.

Here are some ways an accountability partner can help you achieve personal optimization:

- **Provide support:** Accountability partners can provide emotional support and encouragement when you need it. They can help you to stay motivated and focused on your goals, even when you are feeling discouraged.

- **Offer feedback:** An accountability partner will offer feedback on your progress and help you identify areas for improvement. They can provide an outside perspective and help you see things you may have missed.

- **Keep you accountable:** An accountability partner can help you stay accountable for your actions. They can check in with you regularly and hold you responsible for completing your tasks and achieving your goals.

- **Celebrate your successes:** An accountability partner can celebrate your successes with you. They can help you to recognize your achievements and feel proud of your progress.

- **Provide motivation:** An accountability partner can provide motivation when you are feeling stuck or unmotivated. They can help you stay focused on your goals and remind you of why you started in the first place.

When choosing an accountability partner, it is important to find someone who is supportive, trustworthy, and committed to helping you achieve your goals. It can be a friend, family member, colleague, or even a professional coach. Regular check-ins and honest and open communication are keys to a successful accountability partnership. Accountability requires a fair amount of honesty, and some people are not willing to be brutally honest in a kind and compassionate way. Ensure that you are highly selective and transparent. By working with an accountability partner, you can stay on track and achieve your goals with greater ease and success.

To learn more about securing a professional coach to assist you with optimizing your potential, visit TheCOREMethodLLC.com for additional resources and information.

Julia's Path to Success

Julia has always been optimistic and had a growth mindset. She had a passion for fashion and had been working in the industry for years. One day, she decided to take the leap and start her own clothing line.

At first, Julia was excited about the possibilities, but she quickly realized that starting a business was not easy. She faced many challenges, including finding investors, building a team, and developing a product that would stand out in a crowded market.

Despite these challenges, Julia remained optimistic and actively practiced a growth mindset. She believed that she could learn from her mistakes and improve her business over time; she also leveraged the power of optimization to improve her entrepreneurial success.

Julia started by identifying her strengths. She knew that she had a keen eye for fashion and a talent for design. She also had excellent communication skills and was able to build strong relationships with her customers.

Next, Julia developed a plan, researched the market, and identified a gap in the industry for sustainable and ethically made clothing. She created a brand that focused on these values and developed a product line that was both stylish and eco-friendly.

Julia then focused on time management—she created a schedule for each day and prioritized her tasks based on their importance and urgency. She also delegated responsibilities to her team members and leveraged their strengths to improve the business.

As Julia implemented her plan, she regularly reviewed and adjusted it based on her progress. She celebrated her successes and learned from her mistakes; she also leveraged the power of an accountability partner—a fellow entrepreneur who provided feedback and support.

Over time, Julia's clothing line became a huge success. She had a loyal customer base, a profitable business, and a team of dedicated employees. She even expanded her business to include new products and services.

Julia's success was a result of her optimism, growth mindset, and dedication to personal optimization. By identifying her strengths, developing a plan, managing her time effectively, and leveraging the power of an accountability partner, she was able to achieve her entrepreneurial dreams. Julia learned that with hard work, determination, and the power of optimization, anything is possible.

Conclusion

Optimization is maximizing efficiency and effectiveness to achieve the best possible results. In personal and professional contexts, optimization requires identifying areas for improvement and taking steps to enhance performance and achieve desired outcomes. By optimizing your approach to personal and professional goals, you can achieve better results and improve your overall well-being and success.

A MOMENT OF REFLECTION

Complete the survey questions to determine if you are optimistic and have a growth mindset.

For each question, give yourself a score between 1 and 5, with 1 being strongly disagree and 5 being strongly agree. Add up your scores to get a total out of 50.

1. Do you believe that your abilities and intelligence can be developed through hard work and dedication? Do you view challenges and setbacks as opportunities for growth and learning?
   Score _____

2. Do you embrace change and see it as a chance to improve and innovate?
   Score _____

3. Do you focus on the positive aspects of a situation and look for solutions rather than dwelling on problems?
   Score _____

4. Do you believe that failure is a natural part of the learning process and an opportunity to improve?
   Score _____

5. Do you seek out feedback and use it to improve your performance?
    Score _____

6. Do you set goals for yourself and work toward achieving them, even if they seem difficult or impossible?
    Score _____

7. Do you believe that you can learn from the success of others and use it to improve your own performance?
    Score _____

8. Do you have a positive attitude toward life and believe that good things will happen to you?
    Score _____

9. Do you believe that you have control over your destiny and can shape your future through your actions and decisions?
    Score _____

Total: _____

Results Interpretation:

If your score is between 40-50, you have a strong growth mindset and are optimistic about your abilities and future.

If your score is between 30-39, you have a moderate growth mindset and could benefit from focusing more on growth and learning.

If your score is below 30, you may have a fixed mindset and could benefit from working on developing a growth mindset and becoming more optimistic

CHAPTER 4

Reflection

REFLECTION IS A POWERFUL tool that can help us learn from our experiences, improve our performance, and achieve our goals. It involves taking the time to think about what we have done, what we have learned, and how we can use that knowledge to improve ourselves and our lives. Reflection allows us to learn from our mistakes. When we reflect on our experiences, we can identify what went wrong, what we could have done differently, and how we can avoid making the same mistakes in the future. This can help us improve our performance and achieve better results. Reflection can also help us identify our strengths and weaknesses. By reflecting on our experiences, we can identify what we are good at and what we need to work on—this can help us focus our efforts on areas where we need to improve and leverage our strengths to achieve our goals.

Another benefit of reflection is that it can help us gain perspective. When we reflect on our experiences, we can see things from a different point of view and gain a deeper understanding of ourselves and the world around us. This can help us make better decisions and navigate life's challenges more effectively. Reflection can also help us stay motivated and focused on our goals. By reflecting on our progress, we can see how far we have come and what we need to do to achieve our goals; this can help us stay motivated and focused on our goals, even when we face obstacles or setbacks.

To harness the power of reflection, it is important to make it a regular practice. This can involve setting aside time each day or week to reflect on our experiences, writing in a journal, or talking with a mentor or accountability partner. It is also important to be honest with ourselves and open to learning from our experiences, even when they are difficult or uncomfortable.

Journaling is the practice of writing down one's thoughts, feelings, and experiences in a journal or diary. It is a form of self-reflection and self-expression that can help individuals process their emotions, gain clarity about their thoughts and feelings, and track their personal growth over time. Journaling can take many forms, from freewriting to structured prompts or exercises. Some people use journaling as a way to record their daily experiences and events, while others use it as a tool for self-discovery and personal growth.

There are many benefits to journaling, including improved mental health, increased self-awareness, and reduced stress and anxiety. Journaling can also help individuals develop a greater sense of gratitude, mindfulness, and empathy for themselves and others. Journaling is an effective tool when leveraged consistently—it allows you to reflect on your progress, track your achievements, and identify areas for improvement.

Here are five tips for journaling:

1. **Set aside time:** Set aside time each day or week to journal. This will help you make it a habit and ensure that you are consistently reflecting on your progress.

2. **Be honest:** Be honest with yourself when journaling. Write down your successes and challenges, and reflect on what you could have done differently.

3. **Track your progress:** Use your journal to track your progress toward your goals. Write down your achievements and celebrate your successes.

4. **Identify areas for improvement:** Use your journal to identify areas for improvement. Reflect on your challenges and
   think about what you can do differently to overcome them.

5. **Stay positive:** Stay positive when journaling. Focus on your
   achievements and progress, and maintain an optimistic
   outlook on your ability to achieve your goals.

As you reflect on various aspects of your life—including decisions,
relationships, and outcomes—there are a few areas that you should
focus on to determine whether you are taking the appropriate steps
toward achieving purpose-driven results.

Let's explore critical areas that should be considered during the
journaling process:

- networking

- curiosity

- authenticity

- impact

- knowing when to pivot

- ongoing learning and development

Understanding your behavior and actions in these areas is important to forward movement. Focusing on your behaviors during
reflection ensures that you are positioning yourself for success.

Networking

Networking can help you achieve purpose-driven results; it involves building relationships with people who share your interests, goals, and values, and leveraging those relationships to achieve your objectives. Networking can also help you find new opportunities—by building relationships with people in your industry or field, you can learn about job openings, projects, and other opportunities that may be a good fit for your skills and interests. You can also find potential collaborators and partners who can help you achieve your goals.

You will expand your knowledge and skills by connecting with people who have different perspectives and experiences, and you can learn new things and gain insights that can help you achieve your goals. You can also find mentors and advisers who can provide guidance and support.

Another benefit of networking is that it can help you build your reputation and credibility. By connecting with people who are respected and influential in your field, you can gain visibility and recognition for your work; this can help you establish yourself as an expert and build a strong personal brand.

To harness the power of networking, it is important to be strategic and intentional in your approach—this can involve identifying your goals and objectives and then seeking out people who can help you achieve them. It is also important to be authentic and genuine in your interactions and to focus on building relationships rather than just collecting contacts. The art of networking is a two-way street: you should be prepared to offer your skills and expertise to assist the relationship you are pursuing. Consider what you are bringing to the table versus just expecting something in return.

As you are journaling, reflect on your networking capabilities with the following:

- **Evaluate your current network:** Take a look at the people in your current network and assess whether they are helping you achieve your goals. Are there any gaps in your network that you need to fill?

- **Identify your strengths and weaknesses:** Consider your strengths and weaknesses when it comes to networking. Are you comfortable meeting new people and building relationships, or do you struggle with shyness or social anxiety? Do you have strong communication skills, or do you need to work on your ability to connect with others?

- **Set networking goals:** Based on your evaluation of your current network and your strengths and weaknesses, set specific networking goals for yourself—this could include attending networking events, reaching out to new contacts, or building relationships with mentors or advisers.

- **Reflect on your progress:** Regularly reflect on your networking efforts and assess whether you are making progress toward your goals. Are you building new relationships and expanding your network? Are you achieving the results you want?

- **Seek feedback:** Ask for feedback from others on your networking skills. This could include colleagues, mentors, or networking contacts. Be open to constructive criticism and use it to improve your networking capabilities.

By reflecting on your networking capabilities and taking steps to improve them, you can build a strong network of resources who can help you achieve your goals and make a positive impact in the world.

Networking is a powerful tool that can help you achieve purpose-driven results. By building relationships with people who share your interests, goals, and values, you can expand your knowledge and skills, find new opportunities, and build your reputation and credibility. By being strategic and intentional in your approach, you can harness the power of networking to achieve purpose-driven results.

Curiosity

Curiosity is important to delivering on your purpose because it drives you to seek out new knowledge, explore new ideas, and challenge your assumptions. When you are curious, you are motivated to learn and grow, and you are open to new experiences and perspectives.

Reflecting on levels of curiosity is important because it helps you understand how open-minded and engaged you are in your work and personal life. By assessing your level of curiosity, you can identify areas where you may need to improve and take steps to cultivate a more curious mindset. Reflecting on levels of curiosity can help you identify areas where you may be stuck or stagnant in your thinking. When you are not curious, you may be more likely to rely on old habits and assumptions, which can limit your ability to grow and learn. By reflecting on your level of curiosity, you can identify areas where you may be stuck and take steps to challenge your assumptions and explore new ideas.

When you are not curious, you may be less likely to be passionate and enthusiastic about your work, which can lead to burnout and disengagement. By reflecting on your level of curiosity, you can identify areas where you may need to reignite your passion and motivation, then take steps to cultivate a more curious mindset.

Another benefit of reflecting on levels of curiosity is that it can help you build stronger relationships with others. When you are curious about other people's experiences and perspectives, you are more likely to listen actively and engage in meaningful conversations–this can help you build trust and rapport with others, which is essential for achieving your purpose.

Reflecting on levels of curiosity is important because it helps you understand how open-minded and engaged you are in your work and life. By assessing your level of curiosity, you can identify areas where you may need to improve and take steps to cultivate a more curious mindset. This can help you challenge your assumptions and reignite your passion and motivation while building stronger relationships.

Authenticity

Authenticity is the quality of being true to yourself. Being authentic requires being honest and transparent about who you are, what you stand for, and what you believe in, even if it means being vulnerable or going against the norm.

Authenticity is often associated with being genuine, sincere, and trustworthy. When you are authentic, you are not trying to be someone else or conform to societal expectations. Instead, you are true to yourself and your unique perspective. Authenticity allows you to build trust and credibility with others. When you are authentic, you are more likely to be perceived as genuine and sincere, which can help you build stronger relationships and connect with others on a deeper level.

Authenticity is also important for personal growth and fulfillment. When you are true to yourself and your values, you are more likely to feel a sense of purpose and meaning in your life; this will help you achieve your goals and deliver on your purpose.

Samantha Achieved Success by Being Her True, Authentic Self

Samantha had always been a trailblazer. She was the first in her family to go to college, and she had worked hard to climb the ranks in her industry. But when she was promoted to a leadership position in her organization, she realized that she was the only woman in a sea of men.

At first, Samantha tried to fit in. She wore suits and kept her hair pulled back in a tight bun. She spoke in a low, measured tone, trying to mimic the way her male colleagues communicated. But she quickly realized that this wasn't working—she felt like she was constantly trying to be someone she wasn't, and she wasn't making the impact she wanted to make.

So, Samantha decided to take a different approach. She started dressing in a way that made her feel confident and powerful, wearing bold colors and statement jewelry. She spoke up more in meetings, sharing her ideas and opinions even when they went against the status quo. And she started using her emotional intelligence to connect with her colleagues on a deeper level, showing empathy and understanding when they were going through tough times.

At first, Samantha's colleagues were taken aback by her new approach; they weren't used to seeing a woman in a leadership position who was so confident and assertive. But as they got to know her better, they began to see the value in her unique perspective. They started coming to her for advice and guidance; they began to respect her as a leader.

As Samantha continued to leverage her true, authentic self, she found that she was able to achieve more success than she ever thought possible. She was able to build strong relationships with her colleagues and she was able to make a real impact on the organization—and she knew that it was her authenticity that had allowed her to do so.

Looking back, Samantha realized that being the only female leader in her organization had actually been an advantage. It had allowed her to bring a fresh perspective to the table and it had given her the opportunity to show what a strong, confident woman could achieve. She was proud to have paved the way for other women to follow in her footsteps.

Here are five steps you can take to assess your level of authenticity:

1. **Revisit your values and beliefs:** These are the principles that guide your decisions and actions, and they are an important part of your authentic self.

2. **Reflect on your thoughts and feelings:** Take some time to reflect on your thoughts and feelings in different situations. Ask yourself if your thoughts and feelings align with your values and beliefs or if you are suppressing them to fit in or avoid conflict.

3. **Evaluate your behavior:** Consider how you behave in different situations. Are you true to yourself and your values, or do you act in ways that are not authentic to who you are? Do you feel like you are putting on a persona or trying to be someone you are not?

4. **Seek feedback:** Ask trusted friends or family members for feedback on your level of authenticity—they may be able to provide insights into areas where you could be more authentic or where you may be holding back.

5. **Take action:** Once you have assessed your level of authenticity, take action to align your thoughts, feelings, and behaviors with your values and beliefs. This may involve

setting boundaries, speaking up for yourself, or making changes in your life to better align with your authentic self.

Assessing your level of authenticity involves reflecting on your thoughts, feelings, and behaviors to determine how well they align with your values and beliefs. By taking steps to align your actions with your authentic self, you will build the necessary confidence to make intentional choices and decisions.

Measure Your Impact

Measuring impact is a critical component of fulfilling purpose-driven results. When we set out to achieve a goal or make a difference in the world, it's important to have a way to measure our progress and determine whether we're making the impact we intended. By measuring impact, we can identify what's working well and what needs improvement, and we can make data-driven decisions to optimize our efforts.

One of the key benefits of measuring impact is that it allows us to demonstrate the value of our work. When we can show concrete evidence of the impact we're making, we're more likely to gain support from stakeholders, whether they be investors, donors, or community members. This support can help us secure funding, build partnerships, and expand our reach, ultimately allowing us to make an even greater impact.

Measuring impact can also help us identify areas where we can improve. By tracking our progress over time, we can see where we're falling short and make adjustments to our approach; this can help us be more efficient and effective in achieving our goals, and it can help us avoid wasting resources on strategies that aren't working.

Another benefit of measuring impact is that it can help us stay motivated and focused. When we can see the progress we're making, it can be a powerful motivator to keep going, even when the work is challenging. It can also help us stay focused on our purpose, reminding us of why we set out to make a difference in the first place.

Measuring impact is a critical component of fulfilling purpose-driven results. By tracking our progress, we can demonstrate the value of our work, identify areas for improvement, and stay motivated and focused on our goals. Whether we're working to make a difference in our communities, our organizations, or the world at large, measuring impact is an essential tool for achieving success.

Know When to Pivot

Knowing when to pivot and change your approach can be challenging, but there are several signs that may indicate it is time to make a change. Pivoting requires a careful evaluation of your progress, feedback, market conditions, opportunities, passion, motivation, and financial situation. By being open to change and willing to pivot when necessary, you can adapt to new challenges, achieve your goals, and make a positive impact in the world.

Here are some indicators that you may need to pivot and change your approach:

- **Lack of progress:** If you have been working toward a goal for a significant amount of time and have not made any progress, it may be time to pivot and try a new approach.

- **Negative feedback:** If you are receiving negative feedback from customers, employees, or other stakeholders, it may be a sign that your approach is not working and needs to be adjusted.

- **Changing market conditions:** If the market or industry you are operating in is changing rapidly, it may be necessary to pivot and adapt to stay competitive.

- **New opportunities:** If new opportunities arise that align with your goals and values, it may be worth pivoting and changing your approach to take advantage of them.

- **Lack of passion or motivation:** If you are no longer passionate or motivated about your work, it may be a sign that you need to pivot and find a new approach that aligns with your interests and values.

- **Financial constraints:** If you are facing financial constraints or are not generating enough revenue, it may be necessary to pivot and find a new, more sustainable approach.

If you find that these conditions exist, adjust your approach to improve your impact; this may involve changing your strategy, setting new goals, or refining your processes.

Continuous Learning and Development

Learning and development are not only important for organizations to achieve purpose-driven results, but they are also crucial for individuals to achieve their personal goals and purpose in life. Purpose-driven results are outcomes that align with your values, passions, and aspirations. In order to achieve these results, you need to invest in your learning and development. Don't wait for someone to send you to training—be inquisitive and curious; create space to learn independently.

Learning and development will help you acquire new skills and knowledge that are essential for achieving purpose-driven results. For example, if your individual purpose is to become a successful entrepreneur, you will need to learn about business management, marketing, and finance. This requires training and development programs that focus on entrepreneurship and business skills.

Moreover, learning and development help you to stay up-to-date with the latest trends and technologies in your field. This is particularly important in today's fast-paced and ever-changing world. Individuals who invest in their learning and development are better equipped to adapt to changes and stay ahead of the competition.

Learning and development will also help you feel fulfilled and engaged. When you feel you are growing and developing, you are more likely to be motivated and committed to achieving your purpose-driven results. This, in turn, leads to higher levels of personal satisfaction and fulfillment.

In addition, learning and development can help you be innovative and strive for continuous improvement in your personal life. When you are encouraged to learn and experiment, you are more likely to come up with new ideas and solutions that can help you achieve purpose-driven results.

A MOMENT OF REFLECTION

Reflection Exercise: Leverage key reflection strengths to achieve purpose-driven results.

Objective: To practice the art of reflection and identify ways to leverage key strengths in your personal and professional life.

Instructions:

1. Take a few minutes to reflect on your personal and professional life. Think about your strengths and weaknesses, and consider how you can leverage your strengths to achieve your goals.

2. Write down the following six key strengths of reflection: networking, curiosity, authenticity, impact, knowing when to pivot, and ongoing learning and development. Then, answer the following questions:

Networking: How can I leverage my networking skills to build stronger relationships with my colleagues, clients, and customers? What steps can I take to expand my network and connect with new people?

_____

_____

_____

Curiosity: How can I cultivate my curiosity and use it to drive innovation and creativity in my work? What new skills or knowledge can I acquire to enhance my curiosity?

_____

_____

_____

Authenticity: How can I be more authentic in my personal and professional life? What steps can I take to build trust and credibility with others?

_____

_____

_____

_____

Impact: How can I make a positive impact in the world through my work? What steps can I take to ensure that my work aligns with my values and contributes to a greater good?

_____

_____

_____

_____

Knowing when to pivot: How can I develop my ability to recognize when it's time to pivot and change direction in my work? What steps can I take to be more flexible and adaptable in the face of change?

_____

_____

_____

Ongoing learning and development: How can I continue to learn and grow as an entrepreneur? What steps can I take to stay up-to-date with the latest trends and technologies in my industry?

_____

_____

_____

3. Take some time to review your answers and identify specific actions you can take to leverage your strengths and achieve your goals. Write down these actions and commit to taking them over the next few weeks.

_____

_____

_____

_____

_____

4. Finally, reflect on the exercise and consider how you can incorporate regular reflection into your personal and professional life. What benefits do you see in taking time to reflect on your strengths and weaknesses? How can you make reflection a regular part of your routine?

_____

_____

_____

_____

_____

_____

CHAPTER 5

Execution

"THOMAS EDISON BRILLIANTLY STATED, "Vision without execution is hallucination." This is one of my favorite quotes." It means that having a vision or an idea is not enough to achieve success. Without taking action and executing the plan, the vision remains a mere hallucination or a dream. In other words, having a great idea or a vision is just the first step toward success. To achieve the desired outcome, it is essential to take action and execute the plan with focus, discipline, and accountability. Without execution, the vision remains a mere illusion and the desired results cannot be achieved.

Execution is the most important factor in delivering purpose-driven results because it is the process of turning ideas into action and achieving the desired goal. Without execution, even the best ideas and plans are worthless. Execution is the key to success in any endeavor, and it is what separates successful individuals and organizations from those who fail.

There are five components of successful execution in The CORE Method:

1. **Focus:** Execution requires a high level of focus and concentration. Successful execution involves staying focused on the task at hand and avoiding distractions that can derail progress; this requires discipline and the ability to prioritize tasks and goals.

2. **Accountability:** Execution requires a strong sense of accountability—this means taking responsibility for your actions and decisions while being willing to accept the consequences of your choices. It also involves holding yourself and others accountable for meeting deadlines and achieving goals.

3. **Persistence**: Successful execution requires persistence and determination; this means staying committed to your goals, even when faced with obstacles or setbacks. It involves being willing to put in the hard work and effort required to achieve results and not giving up in the face of challenges.

4. **Adaptability:** This means being able to adjust your approach as needed and being open to new ideas and feedback. It involves being willing to pivot and change course when necessary and not being afraid to try new things.

5. **Communication and action:** Your ability to clearly communicate your goals and expectations to others, and to be able to collaborate effectively with team members and stakeholders, is crucial to execution. Communication also involves being able to give and receive feedback and being willing to make adjustments based on input from others.

To execute effectively, it's important to have a high level of focus, accountability, persistence, adaptability, and communication. By cultivating these traits, you can increase your chances of achieving your goals and making a difference in the world. Remember to stay committed to your purpose and be willing to put in the hard work and effort required to achieve results. With dedication and perseverance, you can execute your plans and achieve the success you desire.

Focus

One of the reasons why execution is so important is that it requires planning and preparation. Before executing any plan, it is essential to have a clear understanding of the goals, objectives, and desired outcomes. This requires careful planning and preparation, including identifying the necessary resources, setting timelines, and defining roles and responsibilities. Without proper planning and preparation, execution is likely to fail.

The first step in preparation and planning is to define the vision—this requires a clear understanding of what one wants to achieve and why it is important. It is essential to have a clear vision of the desired outcomes and a strong sense of purpose to stay motivated and focused.

Once the vision is defined, the next step is to develop an execution plan. The plan should include specific actions and timelines for achieving the desired outcomes. It should also identify the necessary resources, such as time, money, and people, to execute the plan successfully.

In addition to developing an execution plan, it is also essential to prepare for potential obstacles and challenges. This requires a willingness to be flexible and adaptable and to have contingency plans in place. It is also important to have a support system in place, such as mentors, coaches, or accountability partners, to help overcome challenges and stay on track.

Preparation and planning also require a commitment to ongoing learning and development. This includes seeking out new knowledge and skills, staying up-to-date with the latest trends and technologies, and continuously improving one's performance. It is essential to be open-minded and willing to learn from mistakes and failures to achieve the desired outcomes.

Finally, preparation and planning require a commitment to taking action. It is not enough to have a vision and a plan; it is essential to take action and execute the plan. This requires focus, discipline, and accountability to ensure that the actions taken are aligned with the desired outcomes and that they are moving in the right direction.

Preparation and planning are essential components of executing a vision. They require a clear understanding of the vision, a well-developed plan, preparation for potential obstacles and challenges, a commitment to ongoing learning and development, and a commitment to taking action. By taking these steps, individuals can achieve their vision and live a fulfilling and purpose-driven life.

Personal Accountability

Accountability is also a critical component of execution. It is essential to hold oneself and others accountable for delivering on commitments and achieving the desired outcomes—this requires clear communication, regular check-ins, and a willingness to take corrective action when necessary. Being personally accountable requires a willingness to accept the consequences of your choices and actions, whether they are positive or negative.

Personal accountability empowers you to take control of your life, build trust and credibility with others, learn from your mistakes, and develop resilience and perseverance. By taking responsibility for your actions and decisions, you are better positioned to achieve your goals.

Persistence

Persistence helps build momentum. When you stay committed and focused on your goals, you are more likely to make progress and achieve results; this can help to create a positive feedback loop, where each success builds on the last, and momentum continues to grow.

Persistence can also help build resilience. When you encounter obstacles or setbacks, it can be easy to become discouraged and give up. However, by staying persistent, you can develop the resilience needed to overcome these challenges and keep moving forward–this can help to build confidence and self-efficacy, which can help ensure that the plan is executed successfully.

Another benefit of persistence when executing a plan of action is that it can help build trust and credibility. When you stay committed and focused on your goals, you are more likely to be seen as reliable and trustworthy; this can help build trust and credibility among team members and stakeholders–it can help ensure that everyone is working together toward a common goal.

In addition to these benefits, persistence can also help ensure that the plan is executed in a way that is consistent with the overall purpose. When you stay committed and focused on your goals, you are more likely to be able to identify any potential issues or challenges that may arise and work collaboratively with others to find solutions. This can help ensure that the plan is executed in a way that is consistent with your values.

Adaptability

Adaptability and flexibility are important because circumstances can change, and it is essential to be able to adjust and adapt to new situations. This requires a willingness to be open-minded, creative, and resourceful.

When you practice being flexible and adaptable, you are more resourceful. You have the ability to find creative solutions to problems and to make the most of available resources. When you are resourceful, you are better able to use your time, money, and other resources effectively–this can lead to improved performance and productivity in your personal and professional life. Your ability to think outside the box and to find new and innovative ways to achieve your goals is imperative for successful execution.

Another benefit of being resourceful is that it helps you be more independent and self-reliant. When you are resourceful, you are less dependent on others for help and support; this can lead to greater self-confidence and self-esteem, as well as improved performance and productivity.

Communicate and Take Action

I have discussed the importance of effective communication throughout The CORE Method framework—I can't emphasize enough the power of effective communication.

Communication is a critical component of executing a plan of action. When working toward a goal or objective, it's important to have clear and effective communication with all stakeholders involved—this includes team members, partners, clients, and other relevant parties. Effective communication can help ensure that everyone is on the same page and that the plan is executed successfully.

Communicating effectively when executing a plan of action helps ensure that everyone understands their roles and responsibilities. When everyone knows what is expected of them, they are more likely to be able to contribute effectively to the plan—this can help avoid confusion and misunderstandings and can help ensure that the plan is executed smoothly.

Communication can also help ensure that everyone is aware of the progress being made toward the goal. Regular updates and feedback can keep everyone informed about what is happening and can help identify any issues or challenges that need to be addressed. This can help ensure that the plan stays on track and that any necessary adjustments are made in a timely manner.

Another benefit of communication when executing a plan of action is that it can help build trust and collaboration among team members and stakeholders. When everyone is communicating effectively, they are more likely to feel valued and respected, and more willing to work together toward a common goal—this can help create a positive and productive work environment and can help ensure that the plan is executed successfully.

Effective communication will ensure that the plan is aligned with the overall purpose. When everyone is communicating effectively, they are more likely to be able to identify any potential issues or challenges that may arise and to work together to find solutions. This can help to ensure that the plan is executed in a way that is consistent with your values and mission.

Conclusion

Execution is the most important factor in delivering purpose-driven results because it requires continuous improvement. Your ability to execute is not a one-time event but an ongoing process. It is essential for you to continuously evaluate and improve the plan and the execution process; this requires a willingness to learn from mistakes, seek feedback, and make necessary adjustments. Without continuous improvement, execution is likely to be delayed or fail altogether.

Proper execution ensures that the best ideas turn to action and create value.

A MOMENT OF REFLECTION

Execution Plan of Action Checklist

Step 1: Define Your Purpose and Goals

What is your purpose for executing this plan?

_____

_____

_____

What are your specific goals for this plan?

_____

_____

_____

Step 2: Develop a Plan

- Break down your goals into smaller, manageable tasks.

- Identify the resources and support you will need to achieve your goals.

- Set deadlines for each task to keep yourself accountable.

Step 3: Take Action

- Execute each task on your plan.

- Make adjustments as needed along the way.

- Stay focused on your purpose and goals.

Step 4: Monitor Your Progress

- Track your results and measure your success against your goals.

- Use data and feedback to make adjustments to your plan as needed.

- Stay flexible in your approach.

Step 5: Celebrate Your Success

- Acknowledge your achievements and reflect on what you have learned.

- Use this experience to inform your future efforts.

- Stay committed to your purpose and goals as you continue to move forward.

Additional Notes:

- Identify potential obstacles and challenges that may arise; develop contingency plans to address them.

- Communicate your goals and expectations to others, and collaborate effectively with team members and stakeholders.

- Stay accountable and hold yourself and others accountable for meeting deadlines and achieving goals.

- Stay motivated and inspired by reminding yourself of your purpose and goals.

- Celebrate your successes along the way to stay motivated and energized.

Final Thoughts

THE CORE METHOD is not just a framework, it is a way of life. It is a way to achieve your dreams, live a fulfilling life, and make a positive, meaningful impact in the world. Work doesn't feel like work when it has meaning and purpose; there are significant benefits for the human experience when individuals actively seek purpose in their lives. Success is delivered through your ability to achieve. I encourage you to be intentional and decisive; create opportunities and network your talent.

The CORE Method has four principles: clarity, optimization, reflection, and execution. These pillars are the foundation for purpose-driven results. They are the keys to unlocking your full potential.

- **Clarity** is the foundation for purpose-driven results. Without clarity, it is impossible to achieve your goals. Gain a clear understanding of your purpose, your values, and your goals; it is imperative that you know what you want and why you want it.

- **Optimization** is maximizing your resources and achieving your goals with the optimal level of effort. The intended outcome is to find the most efficient and effective way to achieve your goals.

- **Reflection** is the action of taking the time to reflect on your progress and learn from your mistakes. You must be honest with yourself and take responsibility for your actions.

- **Execution** is rooted in taking action and making your dreams a reality. You must be disciplined, focused, and committed to achieving your goals. Your ability to effectively execute is the most important factor in delivering purpose-driven results

The CORE Method is about living with purpose, passion, and intention; it is about being the best version of yourself and eliminating excuses. Don't be afraid of failures; embrace them as learning opportunities.

As you embark on this journey, I want to encourage you to stay committed to The CORE Method principles. Remember that purpose-driven results are within your reach—all you have to do is take the first step and commit to the journey. Take full advantage of all that life has to offer; you have what it takes to achieve your goals. Live with purpose, passion, and intention. With The CORE Method as your guide, you can achieve anything you set your mind to—always remember that the power of purpose-driven results is within your reach.

So, go out there and make a difference in the world. Make your dreams a reality. The world needs your purpose-driven results, and I can't wait to see what you will achieve.

For more information and resources, visit TheCOREMethodLLC. com.